SIX SECRETS
OF THE
CHRISTIAN
LIFE

Cover photo by Dave Edmonson
Cover design by Martin Massinger
Layout and design by Bob Vacendak

ISBN 1-879534-05-3

SIX SECRETS OF THE CHRISTIAN LIFE

The Miracle of
Walking with God

By

ZANE C. HODGES

REDENCIÓN VIVA

· P.O. Box 141167 · Dallas · Texas · 75214 ·

CONTENTS

This book is gratefully dedicated to the Christians of

Tabernacle Baptist Church

in George, Iowa

—

PROLOGUE

A few years ago, Jimmy believed in the Lord Jesus Christ for the free gift of everlasting life. He knows that he is eternally saved and destined to live forever in the Kingdom of God.

His initial experience of the Christian life was one of joyful discovery as he learned more and more about God's Word in the Bible-teaching church he attended. God also answered a lot of his prayers.

But now, several years later, he feels bogged down. Christianity seems less joyful to him now and he is struggling unsuccessfully with some personal sins.

One day he bumps into Tom, an older Christian he hasn't seen for a while. After a few minutes, Tom asks Jimmy a question.

"So how are you doing in your Christian life, Jimmy?"

"Well, Tom, I don't know. Not too good, I guess."

"How so, Jimmy? What seems to be the problem?"

"Oh, I guess it's just that it all seems like such a struggle. I have some bad habits that I just can't seem to shake."

"Such as what?"

"Well, I don't want to turn this into a confessional, but one of my problems is that I just don't seem to have any patience. I get really ticked off at some of the people at work, and I lose my cool with them sometimes."

"Is that all?"

"No. There are other things too. One that really worries me is that I don't seem to want to share God's Word anymore. I think I'm slipping, Tom."

"To be honest, it doesn't sound good, Jimmy. It sounds to me like you need to sit down and think about things. You need to make up your mind to stop losing your temper at work and to go out and share God's Word no matter how you feel. If you're really committed to the Lord, you'll be able to do it. So don't give up. Keep trying."

"Thanks, Tom. I needed that encouragement. See you soon."

But that night Jimmy started thinking. *I know I'm committed to God,* he said to himself. *I go to church regularly. And I really* **am** *trying hard. It's just not working.*

Out loud he said, "I wonder what's wrong with me!"

—1—

HOW?

How does a Christian live the Christian life?
By working hard at it?
By firmly making up his mind to do it?
By persevering in spite of all difficulties?

At best such answers as these do not tell us much. At worst they misrepresent the Christian life by giving an unbalanced view of it. They suggest that the kind of life that pleases God is primarily a matter of effort and striving.

Of course, most Bible-believing people would want to add something about getting help from God. But if we then ask, "How does God help us?" the answers might turn out to be very general, perhaps even vague.

"He gives us strength," some might say. But what exactly does this mean? What is the nature of that strength? If it is "spiritual," what do we mean by "spiritual"?

The author of this booklet was privileged to grow up under some of the best Bible teaching in our country. Many godly teachers contributed significantly to his

Christian life. I gratefully acknowledge all of them and thank God for them.

But despite some excellent teaching, I often received the impression that Christian living was in one way or another a matter of "dedication." If you were dedicated to the Lord, you lived right. This undoubtedly contains a large element of truth, of course. But does it really clarify the fundamental nature of Christian living?

I think it does not. At least, not very clearly. That's why we have written this booklet.

The Christian's Dead Body

In talking about the Christian life, there are a number of superb biblical passages where we could begin. But one of the best is found in the eighth chapter of Romans. There the Apostle Paul writes:

> *And if Christ is in you, the body is dead because of sin, but the Spirit is life because of righteousness. But if the Spirit of Him who raised Jesus from the dead dwells in you, He who raised Christ from the dead will also give life to your mortal bodies through His Spirit who dwells in you.*
>
> —*Romans 8:10-11*

Here in a nutshell we have the fundamental problem of Christian living. Every Christian inhabits a **dead body**.

We often forget this. Or we do not realize it at all. After all, we are physically alive. We are not naturally inclined to regard our physical body as dead. But from God's point of view that is precisely what it is.

Paul leaves no doubt about this fact. He states plainly: *And if Christ is in you, the body is **dead** because of sin.* He does not say that the body is dead "if Christ is **not** in you," but rather *if Christ **is** in you*! This describes the spiritual condition of a **Christian's** body!

A Christian, of course, is a person who has been born again by believing in the Lord Jesus Christ for the free gift of eternal life (see John 3:16; 5:24; 6:47 and many other verses). When this happens, his inward being, or nature, changes. But the physical body remains unchanged, the same as it was before. It is still infected by the deadly virus of sin, and as a result is completely unresponsive to the new life the Christian now possesses.

The word "completely" is important here. The physical body does not possess "just a little bit" of responsiveness to the eternal life within us. It possesses **none at all**! In other words, with respect to the gift of life that the believer has, the body is **dead**!

This contrast is clear in Paul's words: *And if Christ is in you,* **the body is dead** *because of sin, but* **the Spirit is life** *because of righteousness.* The Christian is inwardly **alive**, but his physical "house" is **dead**, that is, totally incapable of response to the new life within. A great chasm yawns between these two completely opposite conditions.

On a personal level, Paul was acutely conscious of this chasm. Earlier in his Christian life (see 7:9), he had personally experienced what it meant to desire God's will inwardly yet be unable to perform it through his physical body. Romans 7:15-25 vividly describes the struggle that this produced at this earlier period.

No passage of Scripture more clearly reveals the fundamental problem of Christian living than does Romans 7. Though some have thought that Romans 7 describes Paul's unsaved days, this is not credible. As an unregenerate, self-righteous Pharisee, he could not have had the sensitive spiritual struggle described in this chapter.

In this passage Paul declares his inward, spiritual pleasure in God's commandments. He says, "I delight in the law of God according to the inward man" (Rom. 7:22). Yet immediately he adds (vs. 23), "But I see another law in my members [that is, the 'members' of his body], warring against the law of my mind, and bringing me into captivity to the law of sin which is in my members."

No wonder that in exasperation he exclaims (vs. 24), "O wretched man that I am! Who will deliver me from **this body of death?**" His own **dead body** frustrated him.

It is safe to say, therefore, that we have not grasped the true nature of Christian living unless we perceive this basic truth. If we imagine that by some effort of our own will we can do what the Lord expects of us, we are seriously mistaken. Paul sets forth this reality in Romans 7 with great clarity. Every Christian urgently needs to understand it too.

The Spirit of Resurrection

However, as we have seen, the fact that the Christian's *body is dead because of sin* is only half of the truth Paul is stating in Romans 8:10. The other half is fundamentally good news: *but the Spirit is life because of righteousness.*

In other words, God's own *Spirit of life* also inhabits the same spiritually dead physical house in which we live. And the reason He can dwell there is *because of righteousness.* That is to say, the Christian has been justified by faith and has received the imputed *righteousness* of God (see Rom. 3:21-22). As a result, the Holy Spirit can and does take up a permanent residence in the Christian's very own body.

This of course is true of every born-again Christian. As Paul has insisted in Romans 8:9, "If anyone does not have the Spirit of Christ, he is not His." The Spirit of God, therefore, indwells every believer, even though that believer's physical body *is dead because of sin.*

The reality of the Spirit's presence within us leads to an astounding possibility. His mighty power can "resurrect" the spiritually dead body we inhabit during our lives on earth. This is Paul's meaning in Romans 8:11 when he declares, *But if the Spirit of Him who raised Jesus from the dead dwells in you, He who raised Christ from the dead will also give life to your mortal bodies, through His Spirit who dwells in you.*

Often, however, readers take Romans 8:11 as a reference to **future** resurrection, but this understanding overlooks the context and the flow of Paul's thought. The "dead/alive" theme of verse 10 continues in verse 11 and climaxes in verses 12-13. In these last two verses, Paul draws this conclusion: "Therefore, brethren, we are debtors—not to the flesh, to live according to the flesh. For if you live according to the flesh you will die [i.e., reap the experience of the "dead" body]; but if by the Spirit you put to death the deeds of the body, you will live [i.e., reap the experiences of *the Spirit of life*].

The Apostle wants his readers to know that the same power that operated in the resurrection of the Lord Jesus Christ can operate in them as well. Since *the Spirit of Him who raised Jesus from the dead dwells in us,* God can *give life to* our *mortal bodies through* that same Spirit.

Let it be clearly stated. Paul is speaking to readers **already** born again. So in Romans 8:11 he is not referring to the inward spiritual "resurrection" that is part of coming to life in Christ Jesus (see Eph. 2:5). Rather he is talking about an experience that belongs to Christian living.

Thus the splendid bottom line for the Christian is that, "if by the Spirit [we] put to death the deeds of the body, [we] shall live" (Rom. 8:13). That is, we "shall live" by means of the resurrecting power of the Spirit of God.

Of special interest here is the word *mortal* (vs. 11). The original Greek word, like the English one, means "subject to death." This presents an interesting perspective.

The spiritually dead body which is "resurrected," so to speak, by the power of God's Spirit, nevertheless remains a body that is *mortal,* and therefore subject to death. Thus in these frail, *mortal* bodies of ours, we can have an experience of life that manifests the resurrecting power of God.

The Christian life, therefore, is **God's** miracle in **our** *mortal* bodies. It is **not at all** the product of human strength or determination. It is a supernatural work of God.

That's an exciting realization. The words spoken to the prophet Zechariah are fully appropriate here as well: "'Not by might nor by power, but by My Spirit,' says the Lord of hosts" (Zech. 4:6).

Conclusion

Paul's words in Romans 8:10-13 lead to a significant conclusion. It is this: that if we see a person living the true Christian life, we are looking at **a resurrection miracle!** We are not looking at an experience based on human effort, determination or will power. We are looking at the operation of the power of God.

Therefore the first secret of the Christian life is this: **It is a miracle of resurrection!** In other words, it is the miracle of living a resurrected life even before Christ resurrects us physically.

GOD'S MARVELOUS MIRROR

The Christian life is lived by the supernatural power of God. According to Romans 8:10-13, as we have just seen, living this life requires the resurrection of a spiritually dead body. God's Spirit alone can perform this miracle.

But how does the Spirit of God do this? Naturally, one answer is "by His power." But how does He bring this power to bear upon a Christian individual? This question leads us to another vital secret of Christian experience.

2 Corinthians 3:18 discloses that secret to us. There Paul writes:

> *But we all, with unveiled face, beholding as in a mirror the glory of the Lord, are being transformed into the same image from glory to glory, just as by the Spirit of the Lord.*

Here we encounter the rich truth of spiritual transformation. Obviously this truth is implied in the statements of Romans 8:10-11. If our frail mortal bodies are to "come alive" as vehicles for God's life within us, spiritual transformation will have to occur. And if it does, the process involved will be the one 2 Corinthians 3:18 describes.

We need to look at this process closely.

Looking into the Mirror

The Apostle Paul speaks in 2 Corinthians 3:18 of seeing *the glory of the Lord*, and of doing so *as in a mirror*. This is a remarkable figure of speech that invites our careful attention.

The context of this statement makes it clear that the *mirror* here is the Scriptures, specifically the Old Testament (2 Cor. 3:12-16). Of course, the New Testament was still being completed as Paul wrote these words. But the New Testament is also Scripture in the fullest sense of that term. The spiritual dynamic that the Old Testament possesses is possessed as well by the New.

It follows that the Bible as a whole is the instrument that the Holy Spirit uses to change us. So to speak, God's Word is His "marvelous mirror"!

Some readers will remember the delightful children's tale called "Snow White and the Seven Dwarfs." In it the wicked witch owned a marvelous mirror to which she repeatedly put the question, "Mirror, mirror on the wall, who is the fairest of them all?" One day the mirror stopped telling her that she was "the fairest" and, much to her indignation, informed her that Snow White was "the fairest of them all."

God's "marvelous mirror," however, never fails to tell us that Jesus Christ our Lord is the supremely fair One. Thus in a great Messianic Psalm about the King, the inspired writer declares, "My heart is overflowing with a good theme; I recite my composition concerning the King; my tongue is the pen of a ready writer" (Ps. 45:1). Then, speaking directly to this royal Person, the Psalmist overflows with praise: "You are fairer than the sons of men; grace is poured upon Your lips" (vs. 2).

In the New Testament too, an admiring apostle writes: "And the Word became flesh and dwelt among us, and we beheld His glory, the glory as of the only begotten of the Father, full of grace and truth" (John 1:14). A few verses later, the same writer boldly affirms, "No one has seen God at any time. The only begotten Son, who is in the bosom of the Father, He has declared Him" (John 1:18). God, we are being told, is disclosed in His Son.

Such direct scriptural statements as these exemplify one of the most fundamental characteristics of the Bible. Taken as a whole, the inspired Scriptures are a powerful divine testimony to the superlative excellence of the Son of God. They bear vibrant witness to every aspect of His *glory*.

No wonder that the Lord Jesus Christ confronted a hostile Jewish audience with the words, "You search the Scriptures, for in them you think you have eternal life; and these are they which testify of Me" (John 5:39). And on another occasion, as He walked to Emmaus with two of His disciples, we learn that "beginning at Moses and all the Prophets, He expounded to them in all the Scriptures the things concerning Himself" (Luke 24:27).

Later that same day, to a larger body of disciples, He explained, "These are the words which I spoke to you while I was with you, that all things must be fulfilled which were written in the Law of Moses and the Prophets and the Psalms concerning Me." Then in a profoundly significant statement Luke tells us that "He opened their understanding, that they might comprehend the Scriptures" (Luke 24:44-45).

Comprehending the Scriptures, therefore, requires seeing them as a reflection of Jesus Christ. They are like a *mirror* that the Holy Spirit holds up to the person and work of God's Son. With the perfection of divine inspiration the Scriptures capture *the glory* of our Lord and Savior in all its countless facets, and they reflect that *glory* back to those who have eyes to see it.

When this process occurs, spiritual transformation takes place.

Our Unveiled Face

This transforming process requires, not only a *mirror*, but also a "beholder." Of the person who is *beholding as in a mirror the glory of the Lord*, the apostle gives us one simple but vital description. The "beholder" performs this action with *unveiled face*. We must consider carefully what this means.

The Old Testament background is indispensable for understanding what Paul has in mind. In the Exodus narrative under discussion, Moses had just come from an audience with God on Mt. Sinai. He was carrying the second set of tablets that contained the Ten Commandments. But Moses was unaware that his face was shining (Exod. 34:28-29).

At first, Aaron and the people of Israel "were afraid to come near him" (Exod. 34:30) because of the "glory" shining from his face. But when Moses called to Aaron and the rulers, they "returned to him" and "Moses talked with them" (Exod. 34:31). Later he also talked to the people, but "when Moses had finished speaking with them, he put a veil on his face" (Exod. 34:32-33).

The result of these events was this: "Whenever Moses went in before the Lord to speak with Him, he would take the veil off until he came out" (Exod. 34:34a). But once he had come out and spoken God's commands to God's people (Exod. 34:34b), then he put on the veil again. Thus "whenever the children of Israel saw the face of Moses, that the skin of Moses' face shone, then Moses would put the veil on his face again, until he went in to speak with Him" (Exod. 34:35).

In the presence of Israel, therefore, Moses regularly veiled his face, except when speaking God's Word to them. But when he went into the presence of God, he always did so with *unveiled face.*

It seems evident, therefore, that Paul understood the Christian's transforming encounter with God's *mirror* as an encounter with the God of Scripture. Going to the Word should be like going **into the presence** of the Author of the Word. Through the Scriptures, so to speak, we come face-to-face with *the Lord,* as Moses did on Mt. Sinai.

The *unveiled face,* therefore, suggests a complete openness and exposure to *the glory of the Lord* of the sort that Moses himself experienced when going into the divine presence. Needless to say, we must not "hide" our face from God in any sense at all. Being less than open to His Word obviously hinders the Spirit's work of transformation.

But although "openness" to God is implicit in Paul's text, this is not Paul's main point here. Let us consider Paul's meaning more closely.

The Believing Heart

In utilizing Moses' veil as a metaphor applying to the present time (2 Cor. 3:13-16), Paul shows us the veil's close connection to the unbelief of the children of Israel.

Because "their [Israel's] minds were blinded," Paul tells us, "the veil remains unlifted in the reading of the Old Testament" (3:14). But from another perspective as well, Paul notes, "when Moses is read, a veil lies on **their heart**" (3:15; emphasis added), yet "when [their heart] turns to the Lord, the veil is taken away" (3:16). [In the Greek text, the subject rendered by "one" (NKJV) or "a man" (NASB) in 3:16 is best taken to refer to "their heart" mentioned in the previous verse.]

Paul's point is that Israel in unbelief cannot genuinely appreciate or understand its own Scriptures. Only when their heart turns in faith to the Lord Jesus Christ will they truly comprehend those writings. Until then the Scriptures **and** their heart remain veiled so that they fundamentally misunderstand God's Word.

But for the Christian this is not so. Instead, when the Christian comes to the *mirror* of God's Word, he does so with unveiled face. In other words, the Christian comes to this *mirror* already having that faith in Jesus Christ that Israel so tragically lacks.

Faith in the Lord Jesus Christ, therefore, is a prerequisite for *beholding…the glory of the Lord*. As a result, it is also a precondition for experiencing the Spirit's transforming power.

This point is a crucial one. It takes only a moment of faith to believe in Christ and be eternally saved. But we need to **continue** to believe in Him to experience the process of growth and change. That is why Paul tells us, in another passage, that "the life which I now live in the flesh I live **by faith** in the Son of God" (Gal. 2:20; emphasis added). Our faith in Jesus Christ is fundamental to God's transforming work in us.

Very simply stated, we must always approach God's *mirror* with faith in Jesus.

From Glory to Glory

We must learn one further truth from Paul's rich teaching in 2 Corinthians 3:18. Christian transformation does not take place all at once.

Unlike the experience of eternal salvation that is settled forever in a moment of time, the Christian's involvement with the *mirror* of God's Word is lifelong. As other Scriptures also teach (for example, 2 Peter 3:18), Christian living is a process of growth. The goal, of course, is spiritual maturity (see Hebrews 5:12-14).

(Let it be said, however, that the process of Christian growth is **not** automatic. Peter's command to grow [2 Pet. 3:18] is accompanied by a warning against retrogression [3:17]!)

From the perspective of 2 Corinthians 3:18, the goal is nothing less than an increasing conformity to the likeness of Jesus Christ. *Beholding as in a mirror the glory of the Lord* has precisely this effect. Paul describes it this way: *we...are being transformed into the same image from glory to glory.*

Like Moses, therefore, we go repeatedly into the presence of God whenever we come to His Word. When we do so with true openness and faith, the Holy Spirit not only shows us our Savior's glory, but also uses what He shows us to change us so that more and more that glory is reflected in our lives.

This is a truly inspiring concept of the Christian life. As we move toward our ultimate goal of full likeness to God's Son (see Rom. 8:28-30), God's Spirit moves us onward toward that final glorification from one stage of transformation to another: *from glory to glory.* This developing likeness to our Lord and Savior is precisely what Christian growth means.

But the final words of 2 Corinthians 3:18 reaffirm what we also saw in Romans 8:11. The transformation Paul is describing is not our work but the work of the Holy Spirit. Paul's words clearly affirm that this is a process carried out *by the Spirit of the Lord.* The same thing is true in Romans 8:11. Only the Spirit of the Lord can create resurrection life in our spiritually dead bodies before we are physically raised (or changed) at the coming of Christ.

Christian growth, resulting in change, is a work of God.

Conclusion

The experience of the two disciples on the Emmaus road provides us with a prototype of the Christian's experience with God's Word.

Jesus Himself was the Teacher, but obviously the Holy Spirit was active in the hearts of the two men who listened. The result was that these men learned and were deeply affected by what they heard (Luke 24:32-35).

In the Pauline passage we have been considering, the Lord and His Spirit are not sharply distinguished. In fact, Paul states, "Now the Lord **is** the Spirit, and where the Spirit of the Lord is, there is liberty" (2 Cor. 3:17; emphasis added). It is correct to say, therefore, that the work of transformation in the Christian's life is the work of our risen Lord and Savior Jesus Christ through His graciously effective Spirit.

Let it be repeated. We do not change ourselves; **He** changes **us**!

So the second secret of the Christian life is this: **It is a miracle of transformation!** That is, God does more than just enable us to live a resurrected life. He also miraculously changes us. As a result our words and actions increasingly reflect our Savior Jesus Christ.

—3—

SEEING WHAT WE ARE

The richness of biblical illustration is always impressive. This is certainly true in the example of a mirror that we have just considered. In fact it turns out that God's "mirror" offers us what may be called a "double reflection."

This "double reflection" will lead us to another secret of the Christian life.

It was James, the half-brother of our Lord and Savior Jesus Christ, who spoke of this second aspect of God's mirror. His words appear in the first chapter of his epistle where he writes:

> *But be doers of the word, and not hearers only, deceiving yourselves. For if anyone is a hearer of the word and not a doer, he is like a man observing his natural face in a mirror; for he observes himself, goes away, and immediately forgets what kind of man he was.*
> *—James 1:22-24*

James's statement about *observing* one's *natural face in a mirror* is unique in the New Testament. The *mirror*, of course, is once again *the word* of God that James refers to in verse 22. But what does the reference to our *natural face*, in verse 23, mean?

The Greek of this phrase has often perplexed the interpreters of James. In particular, the words *tēs geneseōs* (translated as *natural* by the AV, NKJV, NASB) have seemed problematic to many. The NIV completely ignores these two words and simply has "like a man who looks at his face in a mirror," while the Jerusalem Bible paraphrases with "looking at your own features in a mirror."

The Greek word *genesis*, from which we derive our word "genesis," can signify ideas like "beginning," "origin," "descent," or even "existence." But another well attested meaning is that of "birth." The newly revised standard Greek-English lexicon [publ. 2000 = BDAG] observes this meaning in both secular and biblical Greek. It also happens to be the meaning that best fits this context.

We therefore propose the following translation: "he is like a man observing **the face of his birth** [= the face he was born with] in a mirror." What does this mean spiritually?

Our Second Birth

It is extremely important to note that James 1:23 follows another important statement about "birth."

In 1:17 James declares that, "Every good gift and every perfect gift is from above, and comes down from the Father of lights." He immediately reminds his readers of the supremely perfect gift they had all received from their heavenly **Father** (vs. 18). That was nothing less than the gift of spiritual "birth."

His words in 1:18 are these:

> *Of His own will He* **brought us forth** *by the word of truth, that we might be a kind of firstfruits of His creatures* (emphasis added).

The Greek word translated here by "brought... forth" basically means "to give birth to" or "to bear." James's statement, of course, reminds us of the similar words of the Apostle Peter. Peter likewise affirms that we were "born again, not of corruptible seed but incorruptible, through the word of God which lives and abides forever" (1 Pet. 1:23).

Both Peter and James, therefore, declare that our new birth is by means of God's Word.

Let us note carefully, then, that God has "**brought us forth**" using as His instrument "**the word of truth**." People are saved at the very moment that they believe any of the promises God makes in His Word about giving eternal life to the believer in Jesus. Well-known examples of such promises are John 3:16; 5:24; and 6:47, and there are many others.

But as we have already seen, God's Word is also the instrument by which the Holy Spirit transforms us more and more into the likeness of Jesus Christ (2 Cor. 3:18). Thus we may say two things: (1) the Word of God must be received in faith in order for God to "bring us forth" (that is, to regenerate us), and (2) the Word must also be received in faith for God to transform us.

This last point was the thrust of the previous chapter.

It is natural, therefore, for James to proceed from a reference to our new birth (1:18) to a consideration of the role of God's Word in Christian living (1:21-25). The Christian must receive it in a proper way (1:21). But this process of receiving biblical instruction must be followed by an obedient response. We are "to be doers of the word, and not hearers only, deceiving" ourselves (1:22).

Surprisingly often, Christians have deceived themselves into thinking that mere exposure to God's Word will be effective for Christian living. They may think, for example, that hearing a good sermon or listening to edifying teaching will make them better. But this is a delusion. The effect of the Word is only truly realized when it is put into practice. We will have more to say about this in the following chapters.

For now, however, we must note that a mere hearer of the word is like a person who forgets what he sees in his mirror. He forgets **the face of his birth**!

The Face of Our Birth

Spiritually, what is **the face of our birth**?

In the light of the context in James 1, it is natural to refer this expression to the only reference to any birth of ours in the chapter—that is, to our birth from above (1:18). In that case, the face of our birth represents what we are inwardly by virtue of having been born from above. A new "person" lives inside the same old physical house (the body), and we can see this "person" in the mirror of God's word.

To hear God's Word correctly expounded, or to read it with spiritual insight and understanding, means that we have contemplated what we truly are by the grace of God. But as we have already seen, it also involves contemplating the glory of our Lord and Savior Jesus Christ.

Can both things be true at the same time?

The answer is definitely yes. In fact, to perceive and contemplate the moral and spiritual glory of the Lord Jesus Christ means to see what we truly are as a result of our birth from above. Of course, our destiny is to be like Him in the totality of our being (Rom. 8:29). But that process begins with a radical **inward transformation**, which is new birth.

From the moment of regeneration on, we have a sinless inner nature.

Christians are often not aware of this fact. They know only too well that they have a great deal of sin in their lives. It does not seem likely to them that they have a basically sinless inner nature. They are painfully aware of the defilement of sin in their inward experience.

Yet the simple fact remains that they can say with Paul, "I have been crucified with Christ; it is no longer I who live, but Christ lives in me" (Gal. 2:20). But if "Christ lives in" us, then that life—in so far as it is lived **by Him**—can only be sinless.

This truth agrees with numerous Scriptures. For one thing, if we have eternal life we have Christ, because "He who has the Son has life" (1 John 5:12). In fact He Himself is "the true God **and eternal life**" (1 John 5:20; emphasis added). That is why, to those who possess eternal life, John can also say, "We know that whoever is born of God does not sin, but he who has been born of God keeps himself, and the wicked one does not touch him" (1 John 5:18; see also 3:9).

In the same sense, Paul's personal struggle with his sinful physical body led him to a twofold understanding of himself. At the end of Romans 7 he is able to conclude, "So then, with the mind I myself [his true inward self] serve the law of God, but with the flesh the law of sin" (Rom. 7:25). "My true self," Paul is saying, "is in servitude to God's law."

In the statement just quoted, Paul's word for "serve" is a strong one (*douleuō*) that means "to serve as a slave." Paul is telling us here that his "inner man" is a slave to "the law of God," but his physical body is enslaved to "the law of sin." From Paul's perspective, his inward nature could produce **only obedience**. But this was hindered and blocked by the dominance of the flesh in his physical body.

As we saw in our first chapter, Paul teaches us that our body is "dead" and incapable of expressing the life of God that is within us. Only the resurrecting power of the indwelling Holy Spirit can overcome this deadness.

The passages we have just cited, therefore, lead to a very important truth.

New Testament Scripture, we must conclude, teaches that when we are born again God imparts to us a spiritual nature that responds only to His Word and will. This inward nature has a moral likeness to God's sinless Son. Inwardly, therefore, we have a "spiritual face" that is like the face of our Lord and Savior Jesus Christ.

It follows from this that contemplating **the Lord Jesus** in God's Word shows us what we ourselves are like at the deepest level of our being. In God's Word we see both **His face** and **our own**!

The Law of Liberty

According to James, the person who beholds "the face of his birth" in the mirror of God's word is responsible to follow through with obedience. When he fails to do so, he has forgotten *what kind of man he was* (Jas. 1:24).

In the physical realm, people do not easily forget what they look like in a mirror. Even if they do, they can hurry back to look at themselves again. A similar diligence ought to characterize Christians. We ought to observe carefully what we are, by the grace of God, in our innermost self. We should carry that recollection with us in everyday life.

What differentiates between forgetful and obedient hearing? We will discuss this more fully in later chapters, but for now a few observations can be made.

Fundamentally, obedient hearing springs from the moral and spiritual beauty of the Lord Jesus Christ deeply impacting us. A Christian can rejoice at the realization that such inward beauty is his by new birth. He can be inspired to express this beauty through obedience. But, of course, this "captivation" of the heart by the "beauty of Jesus" is the work of God's Holy Spirit through God's Word.

However, a moment's reflection will show that obedient hearing cannot be the result of an enormous burden of guilt or an intolerable load of obligation. If such responsiveness does not arise from our innermost self as a deeply felt desire, it remains a work of the flesh. The spirit of the legalist is far removed from what we are talking about here.

That is why James goes on to say this:

> *But he who looks into the perfect law of liberty and continues in it, and is not a forgetful hearer but a doer of the work, this one will be blessed in what he does.*
>
> —James 1:25

It is striking that in this statement James now refers to God's Word as **"the perfect law of liberty."** So far from being a burden, the law of liberty frees us to be what we truly are by virtue of our birth from above (see again 1:18). When Christian living becomes a burden which we must "grind out," we have forgotten what we truly are. Life in Christ is true **liberty**.

Indeed that is the very thing Paul says in 2 Corinthians 3:17: "Where the Spirit of the Lord is, there is **liberty**" (emphasis added). In contrast to the law of Moses, Paul is saying, the transforming work of the Holy Spirit (see vs. 18) is an expression of true freedom.

As we might expect, the Apostle John says essentially the same thing. He maintains that obedient Christians not only "keep His commandments," but also find that "His commandments are not burdensome" (1 John 5:3).

We have all heard preaching that left us feeling guilty and unworthy. But hopefully we have heard God's Word ministered in such a way that we intensely desired to obey it. In the former case, the preaching did not show us the marvelous freedom of God's **"perfect law of liberty."** In the latter case, we sensed the tremendous freedom that comes by acting in accordance with what we really are as people born from above.

But even in this latter case, we need the help of God's Spirit to act on what we have heard and thus to become by actual deed what we already are in our inner being. Otherwise we become forgetful hearers, who do not relate their daily behavior to their true identity in Jesus Christ.

Conclusion

So now we see that God's Word offers us a "double reflection."

On the one hand His Word shows us the moral and spiritual glory of our Lord and Savior Jesus Christ. But on the other hand, that Word shows us "the face of our spiritual birth." And yet these two reflections are in harmony. Jesus Christ Himself is the Eternal Life that we already have within us, and when that life is lived it is Jesus Christ living in me (Gal. 2:20)!

The Christian life, therefore, is God working in our experience what we already are by new birth. It is the mirror of God's Word transforming us through the ministry of God's Spirit. It is the increasing expression in word and deed of what we have become by the miracle of new birth.

Here then is the third secret of the Christian life: **It is our coming to be in experience what we already are in our innermost being!** In the light of previous chapters, we can say that God wants to produce in us a resurrection life that involves transformation into the likeness of Jesus Christ. This likeness is already ours inwardly by new birth.

4

LIVING IN THE LIGHT

As we have seen, the Word of God is a brilliant source of spiritual light. The splendor of our Lord and Savior Jesus Christ shines brightly on its pages. But on those same pages there glows a captivating image of our new inner self that is created in the likeness of God's Son.

Both Paul and James teach us that we should live lives that are profoundly affected by what we see in God's mirror.

It follows, therefore, that God calls us to live in the light of the truth that Scripture reveals to us. That is, we are to live in the consciousness of what **He is** and of what **we are and will be** by His grace. But this will mean living with our hearts open to God's word. Or, as the Apostle John states, we must **walk in the light**.

The words of John on this point are absolutely fundamental to Christian living. He writes:

> *If we say that we have fellowship with Him, and walk in darkness, we lie and do not practice the truth. But if we walk in the light as He is in the light, we have fellowship with one another, and the*

blood of Jesus Christ His Son cleanses us from all sin.

— *1 John 1:6-7*

Let us look at this extremely crucial truth very carefully.

Fellowship in the Light

In English the word "fellowship" is one of those "squishy" words that means different things to different people.

Frequently fellowship is associated with occasions when two or more people have a good time together as they chat, or as they engage in some common activity. Conviviality, pleasure and laughter are often associated with the experience of fellowship with others.

Less frequently fellowship is viewed as cooperating with one another at work, or as sharing some unpleasant task. In fact, more often than not, Christians perceive fellowship in a somewhat superficial sense.

However, the Greek word translated *fellowship* in 1 John 1:6-7 (*koinōnia*) has the simple, basic meaning of "sharing." Needless to say, many things can be shared by human beings with one another, and even with God. In the Bible, when this word is used, the context determines what is "shared."

In 1 John 1:6-7 this "sharing" is a sharing of *the light*. In fact, John has just stated that "God is light and in Him is no darkness at all" (vs. 5). Therefore, it follows that *if we...walk in darkness* we cannot be having fellowship with God even *if we say we have*. The reason is simple: God will not share the darkness with us!

Of course, we are talking about experience here. Naturally the child of God shares at all times the possession of God's life (= eternal life), just as a child shares the genes of his human parents. But children who are out of touch with their parents, and live elsewhere, are not sharing anything with their parents **experientially**.

In the same way, a Christian who walks in darkness is living in a place where his heavenly Father does not live. What he experiences there, he experiences apart from God. Sharing, in the sense John means, must occur *in the light*.

Fellowship, the Apostle assures us, takes place *if we walk in the light as He is in the light*. *The light*, therefore, is the fundamental common denominator of all *fellowship* with God. Whatever else we may experientially share with Him, we always share it *in the light* because that is where *He is*!

However, one might ask this question: Even when we are *in the light,* how can God have *fellowship* with such sinful beings as we are? As born-again Christians we know we are justified before God's judgment bar. But we also know that a lot of real sin remains in us, even in our most spiritual state. In fact, drawing closer to God makes us more conscious of our own failings.

How then can a perfectly holy God (1 John 1:5) have fellowship with us? The answer appears in John's words in 1 John 1:7.

John writes that *if we walk in the light as He is in the light, we have fellowship with one another.* But this is not all. The Apostle adds: *...and the blood of Jesus Christ His Son cleanses us from all sin.*

In other words, our *fellowship with one another* is made possible on an on-going basis by the cleansing power of the *blood of Jesus Christ.* Here, of course, *one another* does not refer to our fellowship with other Christians. That is not what John is discussing. Instead, he is talking about our *fellowship* with God and His with us.

It is important to note that John does not say that *the blood of Jesus Christ* **has cleansed** *us from all sin,* but that it **does cleanse** us (present tense: *cleanses*). Thus this cleansing action is something that takes place **while** *we walk in the light.*

A simple but profound truth follows from this. It is true that *the blood* of God's Son provides the basis on which every believer is eternally saved. But as John's words show, it also provides the basis on which God and we may have *fellowship with one another.* And this is true even when we are *walking in the light!*

To put it another way, not a moment of fellowship with God ever occurs without this cleansing action also occurring. If we think there is any moment when we do not need cleansing, we only deceive ourselves, because there is no moment in which we can claim that "we have no sin" (1 John 1:8).

Therefore, by the power of the death of Christ, every Christian can have *fellowship* with an infinitely holy God *in the light* of His truth. *The blood of Jesus Christ His Son* wonderfully makes this possible.

Open to God

But this leads to another question. What does it mean to *walk in the light?*

Well, a close inspection of the immediate context (1 John 1:5-10) shows that John is stressing the importance of honesty and of facing reality. This is a crucial consideration.

The Apostle warns us that if we claim *fellowship* with God while walking in darkness, we are **lying** (vs. 6). Moreover, if we are so foolish as to sincerely claim to have no sin, then we are **deceiving ourselves** (vs. 8). On the other hand, if we "confess our sins," that is, if we **acknowledge them honestly** to God, we obtain His forgiveness (vs. 9).

But suppose that instead of confessing some particular sin we actually **deny** that we committed the sin, what then? In that case, we are contradicting His Word that has shown us our sin, and in effect **we are calling Him a liar** (vs. 10).

Thus John's discussion revolves around **spiritual integrity**.

It is noteworthy that the apostle does not call on us to *walk* **according to** *the light*. Instead, we are to *walk* **in** *the light!* If we stop and think about it, we could never really walk **according to** *the light* since, as John insists, "God is light and in Him is **no darkness at all**" (vs. 5). Clearly we would have to be completely sinless to walk **according to** that kind of light. But we are **not** completely sinless (vs. 8).

Yet we **can** *walk in the light*. Basically, therefore, to *walk in* it is to *walk* exposed to anything and everything that the light makes visible. In other words, to *walk in the light* is to live **open to the light and to all that it can reveal to us**.

To be sure, a newly saved believer cannot see as clearly in this light as can a mature believer. His newly opened eyes must become accustomed to *the light*. That is to say, he needs teaching! But openness to *the light* is a quality that can be truly possessed by those new in the faith as well as by those who have been Christians for a long time. Any Christian **can** *walk in the light!*

But without openness to God, no *fellowship* with Him can occur.

Benefiting from God's Light

By now we have seen three fundamental things that *the light* of God's Word reveals. These are: (1) the glory of our Lord Jesus Christ; (2) the face of our spiritual birth; and (3) the presence of sin in our lives. All three of these realities are intertwined and significantly affect Christian living.

For example, suppose that as a believer in Jesus Christ I have no concept of any of the ways in which I fall short of my Lord's glory. This is not merely a failure to recognize my sins. I am also failing to really perceive "the glory of the Lord" or to truly discern what I am by my supernatural spiritual birth.

If I look at God's revelation of His Son in the Scriptures, how can I be seeing anything significant if I do not also detect any conduct or attitudes that are out of harmony with what He is? Or how can I be aware of my own true inner nature if I see nothing incompatible with it in what I do or say?

Self-perception is an indispensable ingredient in the spiritual process of seeing **the glory of the Lord** or seeing **the face of our birth**. The light of these realities enables us to see how our actual behavior displeases God. And having learned this, we will need to confess our sins.

It follows then that self-judgment is a necessary accompaniment to all spiritual transformation. Without it, spiritual growth will not occur.

But let us recall what we observed in 2 Corinthians 3:18. Spiritual transformation is a **process**, and it proceeds from one stage of glory to another. It is a path designed to carry us steadily forward on the road toward our ultimate destiny, perfect spiritual conformity to Jesus Christ.

But I do not learn everything all at once. I do not see all that the light of God's Word can teach me in a day, or a week or a year. I do not discover all my failings overnight. Growing takes time.

In fact it takes a **lifetime**!

Obviously, then, there is a great wealth of truth to be seen *in the light*. But since I do not see all of it at once, it is essential that I continue to walk in it day by day. To do this, I must be confessing all the sins that the light shows me. Confession and divine forgiveness sustain my fellowship with God. That is, He and I can continue to **share** *the light*.

As this walk in the light takes place, the Holy Spirit will be able to change me. But if I move off into the dark, the process of change will stop, and may even retrogress, until I return to *fellowship* with God.

An illustration may help. Suppose I regularly go to a favorite spot in a beautiful park to relax and enjoy the loveliness of nature. Over time, I notice the myriad and detailed features of that particular segment of nature. Even after going there for years and contemplating the scenery, I may discover some wonderful feature that had always escaped me. Perhaps a bird's nest almost obscured in the branches of a tree, or perhaps a tiny earthworm engaged in its silent activity.

But if I stop going to this spot, my contact with its realities will diminish. I will increasingly lose my vision of its delicate details and will increasingly lose my sense of its exquisite beauty.

Of course, this is only an illustration. But it is obvious that living in spiritual darkness, as a regular habit of life, would cause my sense of the beauty and power of spiritual realities to grow dimmer and dimmer. Walking *in the light* keeps these realities vividly before the eyes of my heart.

Living *in the light*, therefore, is a fundamental Christian habit that must be cultivated and maintained. Without doing so there is no growth in grace.

Conclusion

The Christian needs to maintain at all times a full openness to the truth of God's Word. When this is done, confession of sin will take place whenever the Word reveals the need for it.

As our walk in the light continues, we can see more and more of the glory of our Lord and we can understand better and better what it means to have His life within us.

Of course, all real perception of God's truth depends on the teaching ministry of the Holy Spirit (1 Cor. 2:11-12). His work, as always, is indispensable to Christian transformation. But He does not do this work in the dark! In the dark God may chasten and correct us (see Hebrews 12:5-6). But the work of transformation takes place only as we *walk in the light*, fully exposed to anything God wishes to show us.

Thus the fourth secret of the Christian life may be expressed like this: **It is living with our hearts open to God's truth.** In order for God's Spirit to transform us and produce in us the resurrection life that expresses what we are by new birth, we need to maintain a responsiveness to the light of God's Word.

5

IF WE ASK

It would be interesting to do an in-depth survey of the contents of the prayers Christians pray in private. Such a survey might reveal some surprising facts.

One of these facts might possibly be that many Christians spend far too much time praying for matters where God has not revealed His will, and far too little praying for matters where He has!

This reminds us of some famous words near the end of the First Epistle of John. If a person has attended a large number of prayer meetings, he has probably heard these words quoted or read more than once. The words are these:

> *Now this is the confidence that we have in Him, that if we ask anything according to His will, He hears us. And if we know that He hears us, whatever we ask, we know that we have the petitions that we have asked of Him.*
> *—1 John 5:14-15*

A surprising number of people think these verses indicate our need for faith. They are convinced that we must persuade ourselves that God is going to do a certain thing. If we do so, then (as these verses state) we will get what we ask God to give us. In this scenario, asking *according to His will* is the equivalent of convincing myself that God will act in a particular way.

But persuading ourselves that it is God's will to do something, and **knowing that it is**, are not the same thing. In the former case, my self-persuasion may actually be a self-delusion.

How can I know what is *according to His will?* The answer is profoundly simple. We can know it **from His Word**. But does this simple fact connect in any way with the subject of Christian transformation?

It certainly does! Let's see how.

Obedience Is Not a Burden

The apostle's guarantee about prayer in 1 John 5:14-15 belongs to a context going back as far as 5:3b. John says there (surprisingly!) that God's "commandments are not burdensome." Obviously this arresting claim invites close attention.

God has commanded us to love our brothers in Christ (1 John 4:21). So, in the opening verse of the fifth chapter, the apostle identifies the "brother" whom we are to love. That brother is anyone and everyone who "believes that Jesus is the Christ," since any person who believes this "is born of God" (5:1).

But how do we **know** when we "love [these] children of God"? The Christian may very well wonder how, or if, he can fulfill this apparently difficult command. (Some Christians are not easy to love!) According to John, the way we know this is not when we "feel" a certain way toward other Christians. Instead, we know this "when we love God and keep His commandments" (5:2).

But then how do we **know** when "we love God"? John's striking response is: "For this is the love of [= for] God, when we keep His commandments" (5:3). Amazingly then, love for both our Christian brothers and for God Himself is summed up by, and included in, **keeping God's commandments**!

But the next issue that arises is obvious: "Is this hard?" It might seem now that **one** difficult command has given way to **a large array of commands**. The Christian may think that this looks harder than before. It even sounds like a great burden!

John therefore assures us that it is **not** hard. He flatly states that "His commandments are not burdensome"! Yet the number of people who have thought that God's commandments **are** burdensome is very large indeed. What does John have in mind?

Overcoming the World

As John goes on to say (5:4), the reason that God's commands are not a burden is that "whatever is born of God overcomes the world." New birth by faith in Jesus Christ is therefore, in and of itself, a victory over "the world."

"The world," of course, is a system dominated by Satan (see 1 John 5:19). Satan works hard to prevent new birth (see 2 Cor. 4:3-4; Luke 8:12). He creates an ethos in the world that is hostile to faith in Christ. We all have seen the reality of this in the media and in everyday life. Whenever anyone believes in Christ, therefore, "the god of this age" has suffered a defeat. In that sense "the world" has been overcome when a person is "born of God."

This is precisely what John has in mind, for he goes on to say: "And this is the victory that has overcome the world—our faith. Who is he who overcomes the world, but he who believes that Jesus is the Son of God" (1 John 5:5).

But how does this relate to the fact that "His commandments are not burdensome"? Let us follow John's train of thought down to verse 13.

The Person in whom the "world-conqueror" has believed is identified (vs. 6) as the One whose earthly ministry began with baptism (i.e., "water") and ended in His death (i.e., "blood"). Both of these historical events (His baptism and His death on the cross) combine with the testimony of the Holy Spirit to bear witness that Jesus is the Christ (vss. 7-8 [cited here without the disputed words of the "Johannine Comma"]). When there is reception of (= belief in) God's witness about this truth, the result is the assured possession of eternal life (vss. 9-12).

Thus the things John has just written in verses 6-12 (**not** the whole book!) are designed to reassure the readership that their faith has truly brought them eternal life. The antichrists denied this fact by denying that Jesus was the Christ (see 1 John 2:22-26).

The apostle has two aims in writing this way. Verse 13 states those aims. They are: (1) that the readers may know, on the basis of the testimony of God Himself, that they have eternal life through faith in the name of Jesus; and (2) that the readers may **continue to have faith** in that name!

This last point contains the key to the surprising reality that God's "commandments are not burdensome" (see vs. 3b). Exactly how does this work?

Faith in His Name

The pivotal bottom line for John is that his readers should "continue to believe in the name of the Son of God" (1 John 5:13).

Although the English words "continue to" do not appear in the Greek of John's statement (the NKJV places them in italics), they convey an idea that is essentially correct. More literally we can render 5:13 like this: "These things I have written to you who believe...that you may know...and that you may believe in the name of the Son of God." [The longer form of the verse, as in NKJV, correctly follows the Majority Text.]

But this raises a question. Since those who had already believed in Christ for eternal life already possessed it, what is meant by the words "that you may believe in the name of the Son of God"?

The answer is immediately given in terms of prayer (vs. 14). We should keep in mind that Jesus taught His disciples to pray **in His name** (see John 14:13-14; 15:16; 16:23-24). So the believer who knows he has eternal life by faith in Jesus' name, is encouraged to believe also in the efficacy of His name in prayer.

But the efficacy of that name in prayer obviously depends on our asking *according to His will*. The name of our Lord and Savior can never be invoked effectively for something that is contrary to God's will. No matter how sincerely we may believe that what we ask is *according to His will*, if we are mistaken, using His name will not result in an answer to that prayer.

What then is His will? The answer is: "His commandments." Of that we may be completely sure. So if I want to pray *according to His will*, how better can I do this than to pray that God will enable me to keep those commandments?

Actually this explains how God's commandments "are not burdensome." If in fact I bring to God in prayer my desire to obey them and ask for His enabling to do so, I have asked *according to His will*. The "burden" thus becomes His, not mine. And He is more than able to produce in me the obedience that I ask in His Son's name!

Thus, by faith we triumph over the world **again**, just as we did when we initially placed faith in God's Son for eternal life. This additional victory occurs whenever I keep His commandments as a result of my continuing faith in His name. Victory over the world, therefore, is the true heritage of those who are born of God precisely because their new life is acquired first of all, and then lived, by their faith in God's Son.

Did not Paul say exactly that? "It is no longer I who live," he writes, "but Christ lives in me; and the life which I now live in the flesh I live **by faith in the**

Son of God who loved me and gave Himself for me" (Gal. 2:20).

Knowing What to Expect

We must be careful, however, not to build expectations that this Scripture does not encourage. For example, when we ask God for help in obeying His commandments, we must not think that from that moment on we will be able to do so without failure. No such expectation is presented here.

On the contrary, we are simply told that *if we know that He hears us...we know that we have the petitions that we have asked of Him* (vs. 15). This does not say that we "have" them, but that *we **know** that we have them*. That is, we know God will answer the prayer we have prayed and will give us what we have requested. But the timetable for His answer is His to determine.

Indeed, if we have grasped the principles presented in the preceding chapters of this booklet, we should expect that a period of time could be involved. For, as we have seen, the work of God's Spirit in transforming us is a **process** that proceeds from stage to stage ("from glory to glory," 2 Cor. 3:18). It is a process of growth and maturation (2 Pet. 3:18; Eph. 4:14-15). God does not simply "zap" us and make us mature!

As is the case with many other prayers that we pray, we must be prepared to "wait on" the Lord. We can be confident about His answer, but we must not become impatient. We must let Him work in us in His own way and in His own time.

When we do this, however, we receive the desired answer in God's good time.

Conclusion

It is strange how long it takes some of us to learn the relevance of prayer to our growth in Christian obedience. It is hard to shake the natural human instinct to say, "I can do it if I try hard enough." But that is exactly what we **cannot** do.

As we have seen from the outset, Christian living is a resurrection miracle wrought by the power of the Holy Spirit. It is He who transforms us as He enables us to see the "glory of the Lord" on the pages of Scripture. It is He who teaches us to see in the Word the true "face of our birth." Without the Spirit's power we can accomplish nothing.

It follows that we should ask God to work this transformation in us. If we fail to ask, we are making a mistake. In that case, we are too self-confident, or we are taking the work of God's Spirit for granted, or we have no true sense of our deep sinfulness, or any number of other reasons.

Yet the fact remains that no Christian can live effectively without prayer. The fifth secret of the Christian life, therefore, is this: **It is an answer to our prayers**. Thus, as our prayers are answered, the Holy Spirit transforms our experience. What we are as regenerate people finds expression in a spiritual "resurrection" of these earthly bodies. This process conforms us more and more to the truth we are learning as we live in God's light.

—6—

A SPIRITUAL MINDSET

In the previous chapters we have considered the role of the Holy Spirit, the role of the Word of God, and the role of prayer in the experience of Christian living. We must now look at how these three crucial factors work together in daily life.

Of course, most Christians have a general idea about how these factors relate to each other. But frequently this is only a vague notion that has never really been thought through. We need to consider this issue more carefully.

It will help us to get a better grasp of things if we think in terms of **a spiritual mindset**. The basic text for this concept is found in Romans 8, the same biblical passage we considered in the first chapter of this booklet.

In Romans 8:5-6, the Apostle Paul tells us this:

> *For those who live according to the flesh set their minds on the things of the flesh, but those who live according to the Spirit, the things of the Spirit. For to be carnally minded is death, but to be spiritually minded is life and peace.*

These words contain some very crucial ideas. Let's look at them closely.

Life and Death

Paul's concept of the Christian life was inseparably interwoven with his conviction that in Christ he had both died and also been raised to newness of life (Rom. 6:3-4). Christians, therefore, should consider themselves to be "dead indeed to sin, but alive to God in Christ Jesus our Lord" (Rom. 6:11).

But as we saw in the first chapter of this booklet, this truth describes our inward being, **not the body** (Rom. 8:10). The body, in fact, remains spiritually dead. Only the indwelling "Spirit of Him who raised Christ from the dead" can triumph over the spiritual deadness of our physical bodies (Rom. 8:11).

In the verses we are looking at now (Rom. 8:5-6) we meet the same life and death contrast that we found in Romans 8:10-11. According to the apostle, *life and peace* come from being *spiritually minded*, while *death* is the result of being *carnally minded* (Rom. 8:6).

Precisely parallel to this is the statement of Romans 8:13 that we examined in our first chapter. Since the physical body is "dead because of sin" (8:10), it follows that "if you live according to the flesh you will die" (8:13a). But since God's Spirit of life resides within, then it also follows that "if by the Spirit you put to death the deeds of the body, you will live" (8:13b).

In other words, our lives can either express the "deadness" of our bodies, or the life of God's Spirit within. "Death" and "life" are our spiritual options. But, as Romans 8:6 makes clear, these options are the outcome of two opposite **mindsets**.

This fact is exceedingly important. According to Paul, *those who live according to the flesh set their minds on the things of the flesh*, whereas *those who live according to the Spirit* [set their minds on] *the things of the Spirit* (8:5). Clearly, one's **mindset** is the pivotal factor.

Furthermore, there is no way to *live according to the Spirit* while minding *the things of the flesh*. The reason this is impossible is simple: "the carnal mind is enmity against God; for it is not subject to the law of God, nor indeed can be" (Rom. 8:7). Such a **mindset** can never be the vehicle for true holiness.

There is no way to produce spirituality from a carnal perspective.

The Carnal Mind

Most Christians would agree that we are *carnally minded* when our minds are focused on sinful things. If

I think a lot about my evil desires, then clearly my perspective is carnal.

But the Greek words translated *carnally minded* literally mean something like "the flesh's way of thinking." In terms of the words themselves this does not need to refer exclusively to things that are obviously sinful. To limit it to such things would be extremely simplistic.

The carnal mind is multi-faceted. We stand in continuing need of God's Word in order to identify the variegated ways of thinking, living, and doing things that are essentially fleshly in nature. The "carnal" approach to life is something that we learn to lay aside "piece by piece" as a Christian mindset develops and matures (see also Rom. 12:2).

As a matter of fact, in the previous chapter (Romans 7), Paul has described what can very well be called "the flesh's way of thinking." He had been struggling to perform the law of God in his own strength (Rom. 7:14-25). And he had failed repeatedly. His strenuous effort to live up to God's law is exactly the way the flesh thinks this process should be conducted.

On a purely human level, it is very difficult for anyone to admit his or her own inability to measure up to God's standards. Such an admission is a blow to human pride and self-esteem. And there are few kinds of pride that are worse than "religious" (or "spiritual") pride!

The cry that concludes Romans 7 is the very opposite of pride: "O wretched man that I am! Who shall deliver me from this body of death?" It is not the kind of cry "the flesh" likes to make! Such a cry leads directly away from self-reliance and self-sufficiency.

It is important to understand, therefore, that the Christian life **can** be attempted in a "carnal" way. But this is always a road to defeat. To truly live the Christian life, the **carnal mindset** needs to be replaced by a **spiritual mindset**.

The Spiritual Mind

Paul clearly understood how to "escape" from Romans 7. The experience he describes there undoubtedly reflects an earlier stage in Paul's Christian experience. Romans 8 gives the solution to the problem Paul faced in Romans 7.

Of course, the "carnal mindset" will never be completely or permanently conquered until these mortal bodies of ours are transformed at the coming of the Lord (see Philippians 3:20-21). As long as we are in our present bodies, the "carnal mind" can always reassert itself. But the continuous defeat Paul experienced in Romans 7 undoubtedly belonged to the past for him.

The secret of his victory—and ours—is **the spiritual mindset.** *To be spiritually minded,* Paul tells us, *is life and peace.* The frustrating, discouraging experience of Romans 7 was over for this great Apostle.

But once again we need to observe that the words translated *to be spiritually minded* can be more literally rendered by the phrase "the Spirit's way of thinking." Thus they are exactly parallel to the contrasting expression *to be carnally minded* which (as we saw) is equivalent to "the flesh's way of thinking."

What is "the Spirit's way of thinking"? Paul does not elaborate that idea in Romans 8. His purpose in this chapter is basically to draw the contrast between what it means to *live according to the flesh* and its opposite, to *live according to the Spirit.* The former is the path of repeated defeat (Romans 7) and the latter is the path of spiritual victory (Romans 8).

But we already know what Paul understood to be "the Spirit's way of thinking." "The Spirit's way of thinking" is to think in terms of Jesus Christ our Savior and Lord! We saw this truth succinctly stated in 2 Corinthians 3:18. The Spirit uses "the glory of **the Lord**" as the means of transforming **us** into His spiritual likeness.

This vital truth underlies even Romans 6-8, which is a classic discussion of Christian experience.

The Power of Glory

As a matter of fact, the fundamental truth of 2 Corinthians 3:18 has already been expressed in a somewhat different form by Romans 6:3-4. There Paul writes:

> *Or do you not know that as many of us as were baptized into Christ Jesus were baptized into His death? Therefore we were buried with Him through baptism into death, that just as Christ was raised from the dead by the glory of the Father, even so we also should walk in newness of life.*

Strikingly, the resurrection of Jesus from the dead is ascribed here to "the glory of the Father." Paul then suggests (with the words "even so") that we can now "walk in newness of life" **by the same means**. That is to say, "the glory of the Father" by which Christ was raised from the dead also enables us to live "in newness of life."

This obviously implies that this new lifestyle is in some sense a "resurrection." This is exactly what it is, as we learned from Romans 8:10-11.

But the next question is obvious. Where will we find "the glory of the Father"? The answer, of course, is that we find it revealed in His Son (see, for example, John 1:14, 18; 14:9; Hebrews 1:1-4; Colossians 1:15-17; 2 Corinthians 4:4).

Then how shall we **see** that glory? There can be only one answer to that. The Holy Spirit shows it to us in God's Word. Thus a **mindset** created by what the Spirit shows us is exactly what Paul means when he encourages us *to be spiritually minded.*

It follows from this, therefore, that a **spiritual mindset** shaped by our Spirit-led exposure to "the glory of the Father" revealed in Jesus Christ is the means by which our spiritually dead bodies are "resurrected" and become the vehicles through which "we...walk in newness of life."

Or in terms of 2 Corinthians 3:18, we are transformed into the image of Jesus Christ "from glory to glory...by the Spirit of the Lord."

So How Does It Actually Work?

So how does all this actually work? How do I acquire **the spiritual mindset** through which my behavior is transformed?

Let's look at the basic elements involved:

(1)　The Word of God is indispensable. Only in its pages can we encounter "the glory of the Lord."

(2)　The Holy Spirit is indispensable. He is the living Agent of change in our lives.

(3)　Prayer is indispensable. We must ask for the Spirit's transforming work, since we know it is God's will for us.

Now let us suppose that I am having trouble living the Christian life (like Paul in Romans 7). What should I do? Let us try to answer that question as follows:

(1)　I need God's Word. If I do not read and think about it very much, then I ought to give it a more substantial place in my life. Regular times for reading and meditation (Ps. 1:2) may be helpful, but the point is not "regimentation." The main point is that God's Word should have a significant role in my daily life.

(2)　I need the Holy Spirit's illumination in God's Word. If I come to the Word without a sense of dependence on Him, then I am coming in the wrong way. Only the Holy Spirit can apply to me the transforming power of *the glory of the Lord.*

(3)   Therefore I need prayer. I must seek the ministry of the Holy Spirit to me through God's Word. I should **ask** God to transform me by His Spirit. And if I have special areas in my life that need to be transformed, I can ask specifically for those areas as well as for the Spirit's general transforming ministry.

Will it work? Of course it will! It will because, *if we ask anything according to His will, He hears us* (1 John 5:14). Transformation is **God's will** for us. And He will do it through His Word and by His Spirit.

We may or may not be aware that the process is occurring. Like Moses in the presence of God, the transformation may be so imperceptible that we will not notice it until someone else points it out to us. On the other hand, Moses went into God's presence repeatedly and, after the first time at least, he knew what was happening. Our point, however, is that this process is not basically an effort of our will. It is something that God does in us and to us. Our awareness that it is taking place is not the critical element.

Naturally, we all tend to want to have our finger "in the pie." We think we ought to be engaged in deeds or activities designed to make the change happen. But when we are exposing ourselves prayerfully, in faith, to the Spirit's ministry through God's Word, we are doing all we can. Of course, we will not forsake the teaching and fellowship of the Christian church either (Heb. 10:25).

Suppose, then, that we are meeting God regularly through His Word and depending on His Spirit to transform us. What will happen? Over time we will discover that we **are** being changed. Old ways of thinking and acting will begin to fall away. A Spirit-wrought mindset will increasingly govern our hearts. New desires will replace old ones.

As the Spirit's work goes on in us, we will become increasingly aware of what the "face of our new birth" is really like. More and more we will act instinctively in a way that expresses what we already are inwardly by God's grace. We will not be "forgetful hearers."

Above all, we will discover a growing love for our wonderful Lord and Savior Jesus Christ. Increasingly, we will be inspired to be more like Him in our words and deeds. Likeness to Christ will be developing in us, and others will see it.

In short, we will be experiencing the miracle of God's transforming grace!

Conclusion

The work of the Holy Spirit in us produces a spiritual way of looking at things. This includes our whole range of perceptions.

We learn to think about God, about ourselves, about the world, and about sin from the divine perspective. This is more than just having correct doctrine. It means truly sharing God's point of view.

I can know, for example, that God's Word condemns a certain form of behavior. But experientially I may regard that behavior as attractive, helpful, useful, or any number of other things. God may need to bring me to the place where I see it as He sees it, a totally abhorrent, personally harmful and spiritually destructive form of behavior.

When I see it that way, I am thinking in **God's** way. It will then be possible to stop doing it.

So the sixth and final secret of the Christian life is this: **It is the product of a spiritual mindset.** It is this spiritual mindset that the Spirit uses to transform us, resulting in a "resurrection" of our present physical body so that it becomes a vehicle for true Christian living. In this way, as we walk in the light, we express in our lifestyle what we are inside as born again people. Thus, too, our prayers for genuine Christian experience are being answered. We are becoming more and more like Jesus Christ our Lord.

EPILOGUE

One evening an older Christian man named Frank took Jimmy out to dinner. Jimmy respected this man because his life seemed both godly and joyful. Over their meal, they had an important conversation.

"Jimmy," Frank began, "I've been noticing you at church. I could be wrong but you don't seem as happy as you used to be. Could I help you with a problem?"

"Thanks for asking, Frank. I guess I'd have to admit you're right. I think my Christian life is falling apart. I can't seem to lick my bad habits."

"Are you really trying to lick them?" Frank asked.

"Yeah, I really am. I'm trying harder and harder, but nothing seems to work."

"Maybe that's the problem."

"What's the problem?"

"Trying harder. It doesn't work like that."

"It doesn't? Then how does it work?"

"It's God's work, Jimmy. He does it through His Word and by means of His Spirit. We can't possibly do it ourselves."

"Tell me more, Frank."

Frank did. He shared with Jimmy the basic secrets of the Christian life that we have considered in this booklet.

When Jimmy came home that night, he took out his Bible for the first time in several weeks. Before beginning to read, he prayed a simple prayer:

"Father, I desperately need Your Word. I need Your Spirit to help me understand it and see Jesus in it. I need You to change me by Your power. I can't do it myself."

He paused for a moment. "Father, I really have a problem with my temper down at work. And I need a much stronger desire to share Your Word with others. Please meet these needs. I ask in the name of the Lord Jesus Christ, your Son."

Several months passed. One day a fellow worker came up to him on the job. After exchanging a few casual remarks, his co-worker asked a serious question.

"What's happened to you, Jimmy. You've changed."

"What do you mean, Bill?"

"Well, you seem to be a lot more patient these days. I can't remember the last time you blew your cool."

"Hey, thanks, Bill. I appreciate you saying that. I've been praying for that."

"You have? No kidding? That's great." After a pause, Bill said, "Say, Jimmy, do you think I could have lunch with you sometime? Maybe you can teach me something about God. I'd like to learn to pray too."

"Sure, Bill. It would be my pleasure."

Scripture Index

ROMANS, (cont'd)

1 CORINTHIANS

2 CORINTHIANS

GALATIANS

1 JOHN, (cont'd)